SUMMARY
& ANALYSIS

OF

BRIEF ANSWERS TO THE BIG QUESTIONS

A GUIDE TO THE BOOK
BY STEPHEN HAWKING

NOTE: This book is a summary and analysis and is meant as a companion to, not a replacement for, the original book.

Please follow this link to purchase a copy of the original book: https://amzn.to/2DiiBCl

---

Copyright © 2018 by ZIP Reads. All rights reserved. This book or parts thereof may not be reproduced in any form, stored in any retrieval system, or transmitted in any form by any means—electronic, mechanical, photocopy, recording, or otherwise—without prior written permission of the publisher, except as provided by United States of America copyright law. This book is intended as a companion to, not a replacement for the original book. ZIP Reads is wholly responsible for this content and is not associated with the original author in any way.

TABLE OF CONTENTS

SYNOPSIS 6

IS THERE A GOD? 8

Key Takeaway: The universe was spontaneously created out of nothing. 8

Key Takeaway: Time itself began with the Big Bang. 9

HOW DID IT ALL BEGIN? 10

Key Takeaway: The universe is not eternal and will have an end. 10

Key Takeaway: There are infinite possible universes, most of which would not support intelligent life. 11

Key Takeaway: M-Theory is the most unified origin theory we have at this point. 12

IS THERE OTHER INTELLIGENT LIFE IN THE UNIVERSE? 13

Key Takeaway: Humans will not likely master intergalactic travel. 13

Key Takeaway: Intelligent life could be the exception, not the rule. 14

Key Takeaway: Intelligent life could have been destroyed by asteroids or destroyed itself. 14

Key Takeaway: Hawking believed there is other intelligent life. 15

CAN WE PREDICT THE FUTURE? 16

Key Takeaway: Quantum mechanics determines only the probability of speed and position. 16

Key Takeaway: In short, no. 16

WHAT IS INSIDE A BLACK HOLE? 17

Key Takeaway: A black hole is a star that has collapsed in on itself. 17

Key Takeaway: Nothing can escape the event horizon of a black hole. 18

Key Takeaway: The information paradox was not solved before Hawking's death. 18

IS TIME TRAVEL POSSIBLE? 20

Key Takeaway: According to general relatively, time travel is technically possible. 20

Key Takeaway: Space-time could possibly be warped enough to travel back in time. 20

WILL WE SURVIVE ON EARTH? 22

Key Takeaway: Climate change will only get worse. 22

Key Takeaway: Humans and science will continue to progress. 23

SHOULD WE COLONIZE SPACE? 24

Key Takeaway: A new space program would spur renewed interest in the sciences. 24

Key Takeaway: The Moon and Mars are the best options, though both still present challenges. 24

Key Takeaway: Unmanned intergalactic travel may become a reality in our lifetimes. 25

WILL ARTIFICIAL INTELLIGENCE OUTSMART US? 26

Key Takeaway: The advent of super-intelligent AI would be either the best or the worst event in human history.. 26

HOW DO WE SHAPE THE FUTURE? 28

Key Takeaway: An increased focus on science education is necessary for the survival of the species. 28

Key Takeaway: A sense of wonder, imagination, and creativity are also necessary for survival. 29

EDITORIAL REVIEW 30

BACKGROUND ON AUTHOR 33

OTHER TITLES BY STEPHEN HAWKING 35

CO-AUTHORED: 35

SYNOPSIS

Brief Answers to the Big Questions is the last book published by the world-renowned physicist and cosmologist, Stephen Hawking. Though he began compiling the answers before his death in 2018, the final version of the book was published posthumously.

In it, Hawking answers ten "big" questions that he received again and again throughout his life. *Is there a God? How did it all begin? Can we predict the future?* These are just a few of the questions he tackles as he presents the state of scientific understanding of our universe as well as ruminates on the many unknowns still out there.

The introduction to the book is written by Kip S. Thorne, a Nobel laureate and professor who worked closely with Hawking throughout much of his career. He presents the groundbreaking work that Hawking achieved with black holes and gravitational waves, comparing it to the breakthrough of Galileo's discovery of how to measure electromagnetic waves.

Hawking's breakthrough was to discover a type of radiation from black holes since named Hawking radiation. It was previously believed that nothing, not even light, could escape a black hole. His work was so monumental, he was elected in 1979 to the position of Lucasian Professor of Mathematics, a position once held by Sir Isaac Newton.

Around this time, the motor neuron disease that eventually crippled him began to worsen. He lost his power of speech and was told he only had a few years to live. Hawking believes this misdiagnosis gave him a renewed vigor for life, each passing year, as he continued to live on "borrowed time." It inspired him to keep working, keep dreaming, and keep digging for the answers to those big questions that exist within each of us.

Hawking believes that we must ask the big questions because they define who we are as humans. We must continue to explore outer space because it brings us closer together as a species and may be the only answer for our long-term survival. In his final work, Hawking challenges the notion of God, offers definitive opinions on the origin of the universe, and opines on the future of humanity, giving his answers to the great questions of our time.

IS THERE A GOD?

Hawking is quick to assure the reader that he has never set out to disprove the existence of God in any way—only to answer the biggest questions that have faced humanity since they were able to contemplate them. When he refers to "God," he is referencing the laws of nature as the "mind of God," and not to any specific religious concept.

While it made sense to believe in a God before science could explain so many previously baffling phenomena like eclipses and lightning, science has since surpassed religion in every area except one: the creation of the universe. Hawking argues that science has won there as well.

Key Takeaway: The universe was spontaneously created out of nothing.

Three things are needed to create a universe: mass, energy, and space. Einstein's famous equation, $E = mc^2$ essentially tells us that mass and energy are interchangeable. So all you need are energy and space. But where did the energy come from? Hawking uses negative energy to explain the phenomenon. When the Big Bang occurred, the same amount of positive energy (and matter) it took to create everything was offset by the exact same amount of negative energy. This negative energy, like a void, is spread out throughout the universe.

Because of the laws of quantum mechanics (how things behave when they are very, very tiny), when the entire universe was smaller than a proton, it could have spontaneously popped into existence without breaking any known laws. Quantum mechanics has vastly different rules from the laws of physics most of us are vaguely familiar with.

Key Takeaway: Time itself began with the Big Bang.

A black hole is a collapsed star with a point of gravity so strong that it sucks up light, and even time. A clock falling into a black hole gets slower and slower until it stops. Not because it's broken, but because gravity that strong bends time. At the center of a black hole, time doesn't exist. The singularity that proceeded the Big Bang—that infinitesimally small point where all matter existed—was, in essence, a black hole. There cannot be a creator because there was no "time" in any sense before this black hole. It didn't exist yet. How could a creator create a universe in a time before time even existed?

HOW DID IT ALL BEGIN?

Before science was able to understand it, many cultures either believed that the universe was eternal, or that it was spontaneously created by God. Once science got involved, the idea of an eternal universe was much more appealing as believing there was a beginning of the universe usually meant defaulting to the existence of God to explain how it started. The eternal universe, however, has been disproven. If all of the stars had always existed, the night sky wouldn't be dark, but would be filled with the burning light of billions of stars that had been traveling for all eternity. It would also be very, very hot.

Scientific understanding of the origins of the universe isn't yet definitive, but it has come a long way in the last century thanks to Hawking's work.

Key Takeaway: The universe is not eternal and will have an end.

It is relatively common knowledge that the universe is expanding. When we look at other galaxies through a telescope, we see they are moving away from Earth. The father away they are, the faster they are moving. This implies everything, at one point, had to have been in one place, which we know as the space-time singularity that proceeded the Big Bang. If the universe keeps expanding and the density is too low to stop galaxies from flying apart forever, the stars will eventually die, the universe will get colder and colder, and everything in it will come to a stop. Alternatively, if there is more than a critical amount of matter, the gravity will pull the universe closer together into a "Big Crunch" which will also mean the end, though a much more dramatic one.

Key Takeaway: There are infinite possible universes, most of which would not support intelligent life.

Our understanding of time tells us that something had to proceed something else—that cause leads to effect. However, that understanding is not applicable to the physics of a singularity.

In quantum physics, the Uncertainty Principle tells us that: "One cannot accurately predict both the position and the speed of a particle. The more accurately the position is predicted, the less accurately you will be able to predict the speed, and vice versa" (Hawking, p. 51).

Because of this law, there are multiple different possible futures for any particle, which change depending on how they are observed. These possible futures have different probabilities of occurring, some high, some low. This tells us that in the original singularity, there were multiple different possible outcomes, and therefore multiple different pasts of the universe also exist. If there is a God, he was "rolling the dice" when our universe was created. As it turns out, most of the possible histories of the universe do NOT lead to galaxies and stars and human life.

Key Takeaway: M-Theory is the most unified origin theory we have at this point.

M-Theory describes these multiple possible outcomes of the universe and aims to discover how many possible outcomes involved the formation of galaxies and human life. There are 10 dimensions in M-Theory, but in our universe, we only observe three (plus a fourth, time). Why is that? Hawking explains that in many other possible universes there may be two visible dimensions, or five, but that three is the magic number. In this theory, the remaining dimensions are curved so small so as not to exist in our perception. With only two visible dimensions, human digestion would be impossible (our very intestines would split is in half). With four dimensions, planets couldn't orbit their suns the way they do—they would either fly out into space or be pulled in and burned up. So while universes can exist with any number of the 10 dimensions visible, three is the number that allows the galaxies and planets and life as we know it to exist.

IS THERE OTHER INTELLIGENT LIFE IN THE UNIVERSE?

When speaking of the creation of intelligent life, many people point out how incredibly perfect the conditions in our universe and on Earth had to be in order for it to happen. Some see this as a sign of God specially designing the universe for the human race, others as an indication that intelligent life is unlikely. Either way, the Anthropic Principle negates these concepts as any universe that *has* human life *already* supports it. The reason we are here is because in this particular version of the universe, all of those finely-tuned variables *did* produce intelligent life, so there is no point in wondering why. There are many other universes that never supported it, we, for obvious reasons, don't exist in those universes. Hawking, for this question, takes the conditions that support intelligent life in this universe as a given.

Key Takeaway: Humans will not likely master intergalactic travel.

One way for us to discover other intelligent life in the universe is to go find it. But even with light-speed travel and genetic engineering, the sheer amount of time it would take to get even to the center of our own galaxy—50,000 years—makes it extremely unlikely. The possibility of warp-speed travel would mean traveling faster than the speed of light, and thus would make traveling back in time possible.

Hawking argues if this had been discovered, we would already be seeing future tourists coming back to see our "quaint, old-fashioned ways." The best bet for humanity sending life to another planet is machine life: machines that can replicate themselves using materials from each planet they land on, creating a life-form that simply replaces DNA-based life as we know it.

Key Takeaway: Intelligent life could be the exception, not the rule.

Based on the abundance of bacteria and single-cell organisms—and the unclear nature of whether intelligence is actually beneficial to the survival of a species—it is entirely possible there is no other intelligent life, but that many other unintelligent lifeforms are scattered around the universe. Intelligence could be a very rare possibility in all of the planets in all of the universe that were able to condense, stabilize, and cool enough to support the spontaneous forming of RNA, which then created DNA, and eventually single-celled organisms, and on to multi-cellular followed by two million years of evolution. Intelligent life could also be more likely to destroy itself than other types of life.

Key Takeaway: Intelligent life could have been destroyed by asteroids or destroyed itself.

Hawking estimates an asteroid could cause an extinction-level event on average about every 20 million years or so, meaning that for many planets, they never had the chance to develop intelligence before being wiped out and starting over. Our last asteroid hit over 60 million years ago, so we're due for another. Another possibility—a dystopian one that humans may be facing—is that intelligent life creates an unstable system and ends up destroying itself, such as with environmental destruction or nuclear war.

Key Takeaway: Hawking believed there is other intelligent life.

It is also possible, he argues, that other intelligent life exists in the same vacuum we do, with no knowledge of other species and without the technology to contact them. As scientists work towards reaching out to very distant corners of space with a message, Hawking issues a warning. Only a highly advanced society would be able to read these messages, and a less-advanced society coming in contact with a more advanced society has never turned out well for the latter—just look at how the Native Americans fared after Christopher Columbus landed. Contacting a more intelligent form of life could be spelling our own destruction.

CAN WE PREDICT THE FUTURE?

If we know the position and speed of any particle, we can tell exactly where it has been in the past and where it will go in the future. Thus, it was believed the future was set and could be predicted as these known quantities were determinable. This concept of determinism was very popular in 20th century science, especially appreciated by Einstein who believed "God does not play dice." Returning to the Uncertainty Principle, however, we know that the more accurately you are able to measure a particle's position, the less accurately you can measure its speed, and vice versa. Without knowing both values, it is impossible to predict the future.

Key Takeaway: Quantum mechanics determines only the probability of speed and position.

The wave function of a particle—which can be measured—tells us the probability of a particular speed and position of a particle. We can know the likelihood of a certain outcome. Unfortunately, even wave function collapses in a black hole, where we cannot observe any particles or their velocities whatsoever. This could introduce further unpredictability into theories of quantum mechanics, which are still being debated and are widely misunderstood, even in the scientific community.

Key Takeaway: In short, no.

WHAT IS INSIDE A BLACK HOLE?

Black holes were first theorized by John Mitchell in 1783. If a cannonball is shot in the air, gravity will return it to Earth. But if it is shot with enough power, its velocity will be greater than the gravitational pull of the Earth, and it will escape. This is how space shuttles function. But the larger a body is, the stronger its gravity and the higher its escape velocity. And so, if a body were so large that its escape velocity was faster than the speed of light, then light would get sucked in rather than escape, and you would have a black hole.

Key Takeaway: A black hole is a star that has collapsed in on itself.

Most stars avoid collapsing under their own gravity because they create thermal pressure through constant nuclear explosions. Once a star runs out of fuel for these reactions, it will contract, and it can then restabilize as a white dwarf. But for stars with a mass greater than can be supported without nuclear fuel, they collapse into a point of infinite density—a singularity. In this, we see the end of space-time itself.

Key Takeaway: Nothing can escape the event horizon of a black hole.

The event horizon is the last place from which light cannot escape a black hole. It is where the gravity is just strong enough to suck the light back in. Because nothing can travel faster than light, everything else must also be sucked it at the event horizon. If you were to be sucked in to a black hole the size of our sun, you would be pulled into a thin piece of molecular spaghetti long before you reached the event horizon. However, a hole with a mass a million times that of our sun—like the one that sits at the center of our galaxy—can be easily approached.

Key Takeaway: The information paradox was not solved before Hawking's death.

For a long time, scientists believed that nothing could escape a black hole. What Hawking discovered is that some thermal radiation can escape (he describes this as possibly due to antiparticles traveling back in time, which makes them appear to be leaving). As particles escape, the black hole will shrink and lead to ever more emissions. A mini black hole, say the size of a mountain, would emit enough radiation to supply the energy needs of planet Earth.

The issue is that it appears the emissions from a black hole can be anything. There is no relation between the matter that goes in and the particles that come out—the information is lost. This means you cannot predict the future, and also that the past is uncertain. Without a certain past, all of human existence is random and meaningless. We are defined by our pasts. That the information coming out of a black hole can't be predicted based on its wave function breaks the known laws of thermodynamics. This is referred to as the information paradox.

Towards the end of his life, Hawking was working on solving the information paradox through a collection of symmetries in the universe known as supertranslations. The closer you get to a black hole, the less symmetric space-time around it looks. The further away you get, the more symmetries, or supertranslations, you will find. It's like looking out at a flat desert all around you—it's the same in every direction.

Objects that break symmetry are what produce gravity; if all of space-time were even and flat, there would be no object to pull in another direction. The fact that black hole horizons carry measurable supertranslation charges may be the key to finding where the "lost" information goes. While this is an incredibly complicated theory that is yet to be fully solved, Hawking relays its specifics with deft simplicity.

IS TIME TRAVEL POSSIBLE?

Key Takeaway: According to general relatively, time travel is technically possible.

In 1905, Einstein penned a remarkable paper combining the nature of space and time into one inextricable concept of space-time. That is, there is no absolute, fixed definition of time, but the time for two people observing the same thing is dependent upon how fast those two people are moving relative to one another. Time cannot be measured independent of position or movement. Time and space can both be warped, and in fact, they constantly are. In theory then, if you were moving fast enough relative to another person, you could warp that space-time enough to travel backwards in time. Unfortunately, Einstein also discovered that the closer you get to traveling at the speed of light, the more and more energy it takes, meaning you would need an infinite energy source to actually reach that speed.

Key Takeaway: Space-time could possibly be warped enough to travel back in time.

Many science fiction writers solve the problem of time travel with a wormhole—extremely warped space-time—that allows you to take a shortcut through space-time back to the past. Hawking explains how through negative particles, negative energy, and the Uncertainty Principle, it is theoretically possible to curve space-time in the negative direction, but he also notes that if someone had discovered time travel in the future, they probably would have come back already to brag about it. Time travel itself presents so many paradoxical situations (such as going back in time and killing your own parents) that Hawking warns against humanity obtaining this power.

While little is still known about M-Theory—the best chance at the marriage of general relativity and quantum theory—the components are there to potentially make time travel a reality in the future.

WILL WE SURVIVE ON EARTH?

Hawking presents the major threats currently facing humanity today: nuclear war, climate change, and an asteroid crashing into Earth much like the one that killed the dinosaurs. Two of these things we can do something about, though Hawking admits that nuclear war is almost inevitable in the next 1,000 years. Hawking suggests that humanity renew its love for space travel that put us on the moon in the 1960s because it is very possible we don't have a planet to live on in the frighteningly near future.

Key Takeaway: Climate change will only get worse.

When the ice caps melt, less solar radiation is reflected into the atmosphere, and the climate warms faster and faster, releasing even more carbon dioxide into the atmosphere in a vicious cycle. Left unchecked, this process could eventually turn our climate into that of Venus: boiling hot, raining sulfuric acid with a temperature of 250°C. With a global population that has ballooned exponentially in the last century, and a planet that is running out of resources, it is likely too late to reverse the damages we have done. Especially as more of the population has access to electricity, cars, and starts further contributing to greenhouse gas emissions. Hawking, though a self-proclaimed optimist, comes off as decidedly pessimistic about the future of the planet.

Key Takeaway: Humans and science will continue to progress.

The picture of *Star Trek* where an advanced human society has already achieved societal perfection and appears somewhat static is highly unlikely. Humans will continue to make advances in science and computing power until computers are as intelligent as humans, for better or worse. Within the next 1,000 years humanity will likely gain the ability to alter DNA and genetically engineer the human race. Whether or not nation-states agree this is ethical won't matter—it will be done. What this means is that those who are not genetically improved will be left behind, likely in a class of inferior humans. Most of this won't happen in the next hundred years, but likely sometime in the next thousand. These improvements may be necessary for the survival of the species.

SHOULD WE COLONIZE SPACE?

Hawking is an overwhelming proponent of humans colonizing space and recommends we make a global effort towards colonizing the Moon by 2050 and putting a human on Mars by 2070. He argues that the amount of money it would take to fund these projects is less than a quarter percent of the world's GDP—and it is absolutely worth it.

Key Takeaway: A new space program would spur renewed interest in the sciences.

In the past few decades, interest in pursuing the sciences has been waning. Hawking argues a new space program—a manned program—would reignite the imagination of another generation into pursuing careers in the sciences, which we so desperately need to solve the problems facing our species today.

Key Takeaway: The Moon and Mars are the best options, though both still present challenges.

Neither our moon nor Mars has a magnetic field to protect its surface from solar radiation. The Moon has no atmosphere and Mars barely does. Water and oxygen could potentially be obtained from polar ice caps on the two rocks. The best options, though not possible with current technology, are Earth-like exoplanets in the so-called "Goldilocks Zone." These planets are the proper distance away from the stars they orbit to have liquid water on the surface like Earth. The closest such planet, Proxima b, is just four-and-a-half light years away, which would still take the Voyager—traveling at 11,000 miles per second—70,000 years to reach.

Key Takeaway: Unmanned intergalactic travel may become a reality in our lifetimes.

Hawking invested personally in a project called Breakthrough Starshot which works with miniaturized "nanocraft" that can be propelled by beams of light up to 100 million miles per hour. It would take this spacecraft about 20 years to reach Alpha Centauri, the star that Proxima b orbits. Once it arrives, it could send back data about the habitability of Proxima b. The technology for this project already exists, the challenges it faces are all solely engineering problems to be solved. Whether humans will ever be able to reach Alpha Centauri, however, is a question for the next thousand years.

WILL ARTIFICIAL INTELLIGENCE OUTSMART US?

If computers continue to follow Moore's Law, doubling in speed and memory capacity every 18 months, then Hawking believes AI will surpass human intelligence in the next hundred years. There is no reason, Hawking believes, that the electrical impulses that make up computers couldn't become superior at processing information than the electrical impulses that make up our human brains.

Key Takeaway: The advent of super-intelligent AI would be either the best or the worst event in human history.

The real threat in AI is not that it becomes sentient and aims to destroy us, but rather that its goals aren't properly aligned with our own. For instance, if we ask AI to solve global warming, it may very well wipe humanity off the planet as a perfectly reasonable solution to that problem. We must be extremely careful and judicious as we develop AI to incorporate thorough risk assessment at all stages.

Once AI becomes hyper-intelligent, it will be able to improve itself exponentially, making faster and better versions—its intelligence will make human intelligence comparable to a snail's.

There are many potential benefits to AI like curing diseases, expanding education, reducing motor vehicle deaths, and making human life better—to name a few close on the horizon. But for every way we allow AI to penetrate our lives, we must be keenly aware of the potential consequences.

HOW DO WE SHAPE THE FUTURE?

In his final chapter, Hawking calls to humanity to reconnect with the importance of science in our daily lives. He sees a trend of anti-intellectualism, a revolt against experts, and increased nationalism as threats to the sciences and to human progress as a whole. Closing borders and cutting funding for scientific programs will only slow our progress when we need scientists now more than ever.

Key Takeaway: An increased focus on science education is necessary for the survival of the species.

With global warming, mass deforestation, the threat of nuclear Armageddon, rapid extinction of other species, the degradation of the ocean, and a massively increasing human population, the need for scientific innovation is greater than ever before. We need scientists to solve these problems, but more than that, we need the average member of the population to understand the science behind how our world works. Anti-intellectualism could mean that problems like global warming go ignored until it's too late.

Hawking reiterates the need for humans to colonize space in order to remedy the increasing stress we are putting on the limited resources of our planet.

Key Takeaway: A sense of wonder, imagination, and creativity are also necessary for survival.

Beyond being a genius in his time and the next, Einstein was a creative thinker. He wasn't bound by the rules of rote memorization or the existing body of science at the time. Hawking begs the reader to explore their curiosity, to learn more about as many things as they can, and to never stop questioning what the universe may hold.

In the past 100 years, science has grown more than anyone could have possibly predicted. In fact, many of the inventions that are commonplace today—like drones, smart phones, and social media—would have been unfathomable just a few generations ago. With that in mind, the next few generations are sure to take us places we'd never thought we could go and show us innovation we couldn't even imagine today.

We're going to continue to develop, to innovate, to get smarter, and to build computers that get smarter too. The important thing is we never stop creating, we never stop learning, and we never stop trying to make our planet a better place.

EDITORIAL REVIEW

Stephen Hawking's final book is a thoughtful and insightful look into some of the biggest questions that face humanity. While the first six questions look towards issues science may already be able to answer (at least to some degree), the last four questions focus on Hawking's outlook for the future of humanity, Earth, and our civilization.

Before his death in 2018, Hawking was likely the most renowned living physicist and cosmologist on the planet. His name was a household one—rare for any scientist—though he attributes much of his fame to the fact that he lived his life and continued his work despite his disability. His iconic computerized voice (which he says he grew to hear as his own voice, despite its American accent) was instantly recognizable to almost anyone.

Though Hawking's work in theoretical physics was extraordinarily complicated and likely beyond the comprehension of the average person, his writing in this book is quite the opposite. It is easily accessible, rich with simple, understandable metaphor, and it allows the layman reader to understand at least the basic structures of the science he discusses—even if one will never truly understand the forces and calculations behind it.

One of his goals, as he states in his final chapter, is to make science more accessible to everyone; to help people believe that they can understand it rather than being scared of feeling stupid and avoiding it altogether. In that, his book is a massive success. He somehow takes concepts as complicated as wave probability function in the Uncertainty Principle and the information paradox of black holes and makes them instantly understandable. This summary in itself was difficult to write as so much of his writing was already perfectly succinct for the complexity of the concepts he addressed.

While some of the book is repetitive—due to the fact that these answers were compiled over the years as he was asked the same questions again and again—the repetitive parts likely bear repeating. He covers the Uncertainty Principle multiple times as it relates both to the beginning of the universe as well as to our ability, or lack thereof, to ever predict the future. He returns again and again to humanity's need to colonize space in order to address the problems that he sees as inevitably destroying planet Earth sometime in the not-so-distant future.

While religious folk may be off put by his unequivocal denunciation of the existence of God, his reasoning is sound as far as the science is concerned. And you have to give a dying man credit for being so bold as to say definitively that there is no judgment about to come for him.

Hawking was an endless seeker of information who worked tirelessly, and succeeded, in solving some of the biggest problems and questions that have faced our universe and the science behind them. Though he died before fully figuring out M-Theory, the true relation between quantum mechanics and the laws of physics, before solving the information paradox, his contributions to science and society will make him one of the most remembered, beloved, and respect scientists in human history. This book is a wonderful vehicle for his final parting words, his last bit of knowledge to leave with the inhabitants of planet Earth.

BACKGROUND ON AUTHOR

Stephen Hawking (1942–2018) is regarded as one of the most brilliant theoretical physicists in history. Hawking was an English cosmologist, physicist, and author, who was director of research at the Centre for Theoretical Cosmology at the University of Cambridge at the time of his death. He was the Lucasian Professor of Mathematics at the University of Cambridge between 1979 and 2009. He dedicated most of his life's work towards studying black holes and relativity, and his discovery of Hawking radiation from black holes earned him a spot as a fellow of the Royal Society (FRS).

Hawking pursued his undergraduate studies at University College, Oxford and was, for the most part, a lazy student. He narrowly received the first-class degree he needed to pursue his PhD in cosmology at the University of Cambridge, beginning his graduate studies in 1962. When Hawking was 21, he was diagnosed with ALS, a motor neuron disease that would progress over his lifetime, paralyzing him and stealing his ability to speak. He was originally given only two years to live by doctors, but he went on to live more than fifty after his diagnosis.

In 1988, Hawking published *A Brief History of Time*, a book on cosmology, the origin of the universe, and phenomena such as the Big Bang and black holes, that was designed for the layman reader with no knowledge of general relativity or quantum mechanics. The book became an international bestseller and sold more than 10 million copies in 20 years.

By 2001, it had been translated into 35 languages and earned Hawking international recognition.

Hawking was a lifetime member of the Pontifical Academy of Sciences, and a recipient of the Presidential Medal of Freedom, the highest civilian award in the United States. In 2002, Hawking was ranked number 25 in the BBC's poll of the 100 Greatest Britons. He received myriad other awards and accolades for his work throughout his life.

Stephen Hawing died at the age of 76, survived by his three children, Robert, Lucy, and Timothy, and two ex-wives. In 2014, the memoirs of his first wife, Jane, were made into a movie starring Eddie Redmayne as Hawking called *The Theory of Everything*, which was nominated for numerous Oscars including Best Picture and won for Best Actor. Hawking has praised Redmayne's portrayal of him and of his disease in the movie saying, "At times, I thought he was me." Following the movie, Redmayne and Hawking remained friends, and the actor even wrote a posthumous foreword to this book.

Stephen Hawking's physical remains are buried in Westminster Abbey next to those of Sir Isaac Newton.

OTHER TITLES BY STEPHEN HAWKING

A Brief History of Time (1988)

Black Holes and Baby Universes and Other Essays (1993)

The Universe in a Nutshell (2001)

On the Shoulders of Giants (2002)

God Created the Integers: The Mathematical Breakthroughs That Changed History (2005)

The Dreams That Stuff Is Made of: The Most Astounding Papers of Quantum Physics and How They Shook the Scientific World (2011)

My Brief History (2013)

Brief Answers to the Big Questions (2018)

CO-AUTHORED:

The Nature of Space and Time (with Roger Penrose) (1996)

The Large, the Small and the Human Mind (with Roger Penrose, Abner Shimony and Nancy Cartwright) (1997)

The Future of Spacetime (with Kip Thorne, Igor Novikov, Timothy Ferris and introduction by Alan Lightman, Richard H. Price) (2002)

A Briefer History of Time (with Leonard Mlodinow) (2005)

The Grand Design (with Leonard Mlodinow) (2010)

If you enjoyed this ZIP Reads publication, we encourage you to purchase a copy of <u>the original book.</u>

We'd also love an honest review on Amazon.com!

Want **FREE** book summaries delivered weekly? Sign up for our email list and get notified of all our new releases, free promos, and $0.99 deals!

No spam, just books.

Sign up at <u>http://zipreads.co</u>

ZIPREADS

Made in the USA
Middletown, DE
24 December 2018